Mom's Book

by Cecilia Winters
illustrated by Susan Lexa

Core Decodable 95

McGraw Hill Education

Bothell, WA • Chicago, IL • Columbus, OH • New York, NY

MHEonline.com

Send all inquiries to:
McGraw-Hill Education
8787 Orion Place
Columbus, OH 43240

ISBN: 978-0-02-145005-3
MHID: 0-02-145005-6

Printed in the United States of America.

7 8 9 LCR 25 24 23

Mom looked at a book.

"Is that book good?" asked Luke.

Mom smiled.

"I like it," said Mom. "The truth is I made it."

"You did?" asked Luke.

"When I was a girl," said Mom, "I was on a trip. This book tells what I did."

"I went camping," said Mom. "I was with my mom and dad. We took a van."

Mom showed Luke a page.

"I drew a map," said Mom. "It shows the way."

"The trip was in June," said Mom. "I said that it was hot. But it was cool at night."

"We had a new tent," said Mom. "It was dark blue. I drew that, too."

"Did you cook food?" asked Luke.

"Yes," Mom grinned. "I made bad stew!"

"I threw in too much salt. Three big spoons," Mom said.

Her grin grew bigger.

"The trip was fun," said Mom. "I even spotted a moose."

"A moose!" said Luke.

"Yes," said Mom. "There is the proof."
A snapshot was glued to a page.

Just then Dad walked in. He had a new book.

"This is for you, Luke," said Dad.

The book had blank pages.

"You can fill those on a trip this June," said Mom.

"A camping trip?" asked Luke.

"Yes," said Mom. "You can make a book, too."